This book belongs to

....

About Katha

Katha, a nonprofit organization founded in 1988, works in the literacy to literature continuum. We work with slum communities and municipal corporation schools to ensure that every child learns to read for fun and at grade level. We also work with women and teachers so that all children achieve their potential.

Our books, workshops and learning centres strive to forge cross-cultural connections through story and Story Pedagogy©. As one of India's finest publishers, our initiative has been recognized as "a unique and special moment in Indian publishing history" by The Economic Times.

Katha's books have received global recognition, including the nomination by an international jury for the prestigious Astrid Lindgren Award, the world's biggest prize for children's literature.

We love to work with new and established writers, translators and illustrators.

Do you like writing, illustrating, translating for children? Write to us at **editors@katha.org** to become a cherished member of the Katha family!

"[Katha] ... an educational jewel in India's crown."
　　　　　　　　　　　　　— **Naoyuki Shinohara, Deputy Managing Director, International Monetary Fund**

"Katha stands as an exemplar for all the creative projects around the world that grapple with ordinary and dramatic misery in cities." 　　　　　　　　— **Charles Landry, The Art of City Making**

"Katha has a real soft corner for kids. Which is why it ... create[s] such gorgeous picture books for children."
　　　　　　　　　　　　　　　　　　　　　　　　　　　　— **Time Out**

"Katha's work is driven by the idea that children can bring change to their communities that is sustainable and real, just as the children do in [their books]." 　　　　　　— **Papertigers**

The Friday Fair

Rabindranath Tagore

Art by **Debasmita Dasgupta**

Translated from Bangla
by Himanjali Sankar and Geeta Dharmarajan

ⓘ KATHA

Here comes the cart with pots and pans,
from the village potters' lane.

Bansi rides the cart with flair,
nephew Madan by his side.

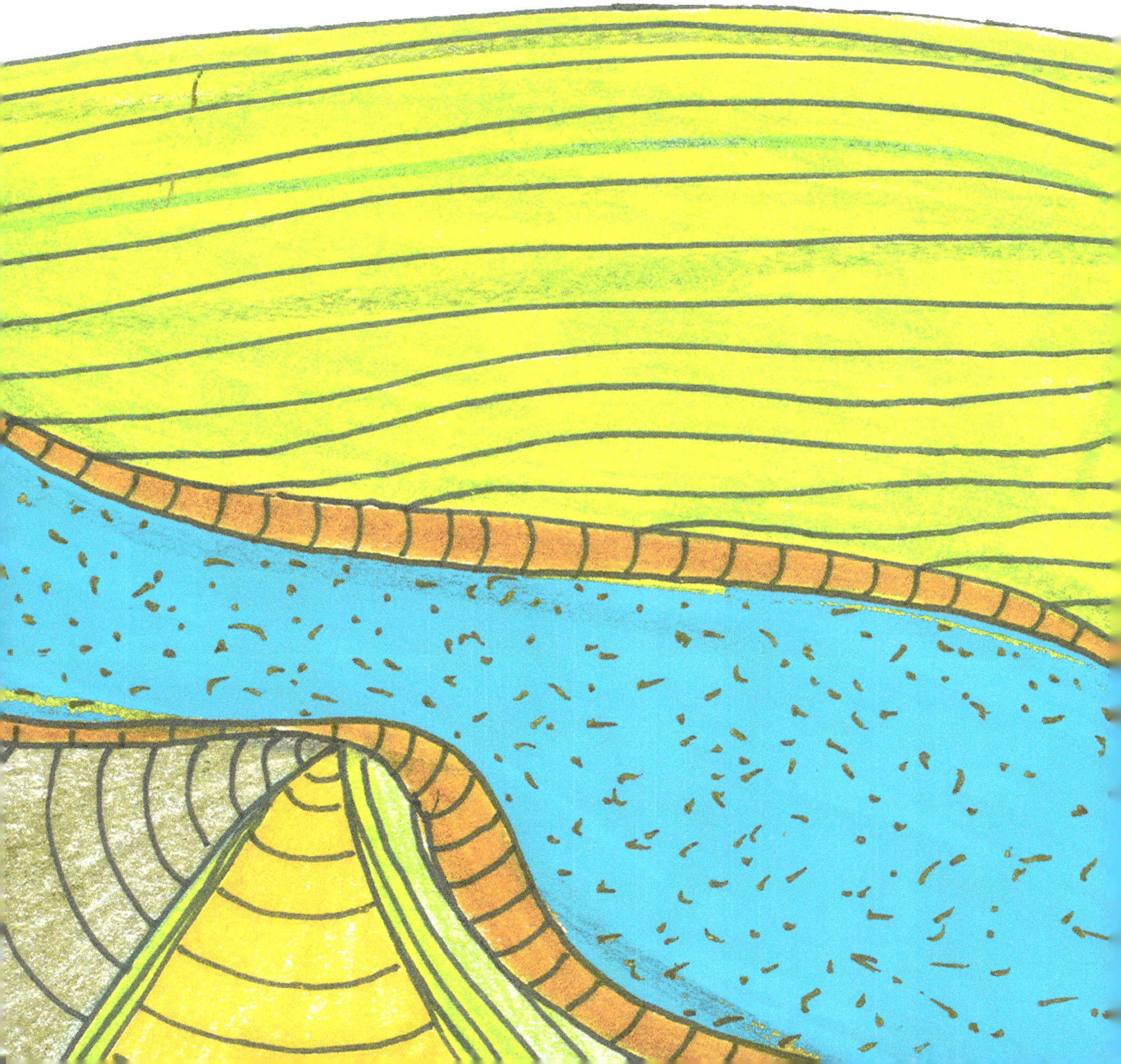

Friday haat comes every week to Bakshiganj on Padma's banks.

People bring the cash they have,
to barter, haggle, buy and sell!

Brinjal, radish, gourds and all,
flour and mustard, wheat and gram.

Delicate winnows made of cane,
handmade shawls so warm and nice.

Ladles, mashers, rolling pins,
cheap umbrellas, tongs and things.

Flies buzz and swirl near piles of gud,
they dance on top of mishti too!

Now see the happy farmer girl,
riding a boat that's full of hay.

And there sings homeless blind Kanhai, softly sweetly for his food.

He doesn't see the laughing boys,
who kick-splash in the nearby pond.

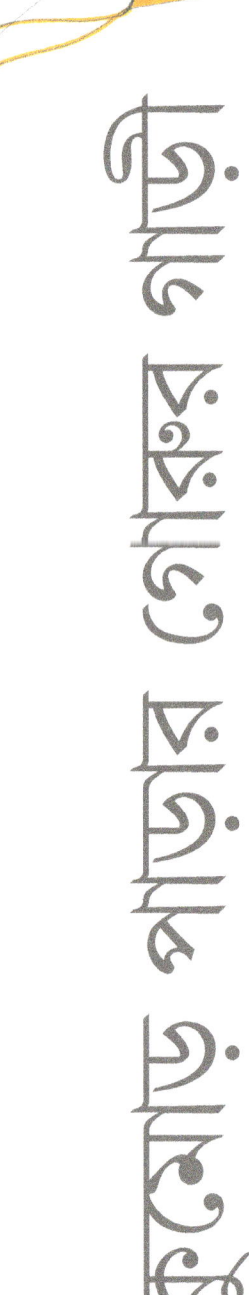

কুমোড় পাড়ার গোরুর গাড়ী
বোঝাই করা কলসি হাঁড়ি

গাড়ি চালায় বংশীবদন
সঙ্গে যে যায় ভাগ্নে মদন

হাট বসেছে শুক্রবারে
বক্সীগঞ্জে পদ্মাপারে

জিনিসপত্র জুটিয়ে এনে
গ্রামের মানুষ বেচে কেনে

উচ্ছে বেগুন পটল মুলো
বেতের বোনা ধামা কূলো

সর্ষে ছোলা ময়দা আটা
শীতের র‍্যাপার নক্সাকাটা

ঝাঁঝরি কড়ি বেড়ি হাতা
শহর থেকে শস্তা ছাতা

কলসী ভরা এখো গুড়ে
মাছি যত বেড়ায় উড়ে

খড়ের আঁটি নৌকা বেয়ে
আনল ঘাটে চাষীর মেয়ে

অন্ধ কানাই পথের পরে
গান শুনিয়ে ভিক্ষে করে

পাড়ার ছেলে স্নানের ঘাটে
জল ছিটিয়ে সাঁতার কাটে

Kumor paarar gorur gadi

Kumor paarar gorur gadi
Bojhai kora kolshi haanri

Gadi chaalaey bongshi bodon
Shonge je jaae bhagne modon

Haath bosheche shukrobaare
Bokshi gaunje padma pare

Jinishpautro jutiye aene
Graamer manoosh beche kene

Ucche begun potol mu-lo
Beter bona dhama ku-lo

Shorshe chola moyda aata
Sheeter reypar nauksha kaata

Jhanjhri kodi baedi haathe
Shohaar theke shausta chaata

Kolshi bhora aekho gu-re
Maachi jautto baedaaye u-re

Khaurer aantee nauka beyyey
Aanlo ghaate chashir meyyey

Aaundho kaanai pather paure
Gaan shuniye bhikhhe kaure

Paarar chele snaaner ghaate
Jol chitiye shaataar kaate

This poem has been taken from Rabindranath Tagore's book, *Simple Lessons*. This book is an important primer for kids who want to learn the Bangla language. Full of rhyme and rhythm and fascinatingly illustrated by Nandalal Basu, this book encourages kids to look at nature in a new way.

Know Gurudev

Do you know which famous poet wrote the Indian national anthem Jana Gana Mana?

Born 150 years ago, he stood tall in the world of writing and his ideas are still so fresh, so current. He was a writer, painter, musician, poet and storyteller too! Yes, we are talking of Rabindranath Tagore, lovingly called Gurudev.

Gurudev was born on May 7, 1861. His father, Debendranath Tagore, was a Sanskrit scholar.

Gurudev's early education was imparted at home. In school, while others used to learn their lessons, he would slip into an exciting world of dreams. Hoping that his tutor would not come when it rained, he would sit by the window waiting. However as fate would have it his tutor's umbrella could be seen right from the corner of the road at the usual time.

Tagore wrote his first poem when he was eight. At the age of sixteen, his first book of poems was published. Aside from words and drama, his other great love was music. He composed more than two thousand songs, both the music and lyrics. He held great love and respect for children. His first poem for children was The Rainy Day.

Since childhood he loved and appreciated nature. Tagore felt that learning should be based on real life experiences and wanted to spread this message. He always believed that education is the freedom of imagination. In 1901, he founded an international university called Shantiniketan or Abode of Peace, which brought out priceless talents like Indira Gandhi, Satyajit Ray and Amartya Sen.

He has also written Aamaar Saunar Bangla, the national anthem for Bangladesh. In appreciation of all his work, Gandhiji lovingly gave him the title, Gurudev. In his last days he developed an interest in painting. In 1913 he was awarded the Nobel Prize in Literature.

Debasmita Dasgupta does social campaigns for nonprofit organizations. She loves illustrating for children's books and has a special interest in cinema, theatre and music. Currently she lives in Singapore.

Himanjali Sankar did her MPhil in English Literature from JNU. She is a senior editor with a children's publishing house and has written two children's books, *The Magical Adventures of Skinny Scribbles* and *The Stupendous Timetelling Superdog*.

Geeta Dharmarajan loves writing stories for children. She was earlier one of the editors of *Target*, a magazine for children and *The Pennsylvania Gazette*, the magazine of University of Pennsylvania. She is the Chairman of the National Bal Bhavan. She has been awarded the prestigious Padma Shri in 2012, for her distinguished service in Literature and Education.

KATHA

First published © Katha, 2013
Copyright © Katha, 2013
Text copyright © Katha, 2013
Illustrations copyright © Debasmita Dasgupta, 2011
All rights reserved. No part of this book may be reproduced or utilized in any form without the prior written permission of the publisher.
ISBN 978-93-82454-10-6
E-mail: marketing@katha.org, Website: www.katha.org

KATHA is a registered nonprofit organization devoted to enhancing the joys of reading amongst children and adults. Katha Schools are situated in the slums and streets of Delhi and tribal villages of Arunachal Pradesh.
A3 Sarvodaya Enclave, Sri Aurobindo Marg, New Delhi 110 017
Phone: 4141 6600 . 4182 9998 . 2652 1752
Fax: 2651 4373

English Translation: Himanjali Sankar and Geeta Dharmarajan

Ten per cent of sales proceeds from this book will support the quality education of children studying in Katha schools.
Katha regularly plants trees to replace the wood used in the making of its books.

Tantalizing Tagore!
The other books in the series

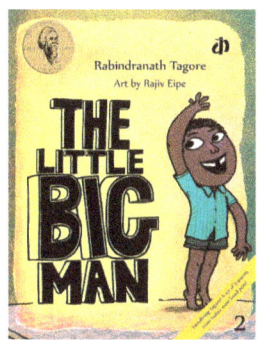

The Little Big Man
Art by Rajiv Eipe

The Little Big Man shows what it's like for a child to wear his father's shoes, to grow up and assume adult responsibilities. Through the eyes of a child, a poetic ideal!

"The artwork by Rajiv Eipe perfectly compliments the text. The little boy with front tooth missing looks absolutely endearing in his expression of – all grown up and responsible." — **Saffron Tree**

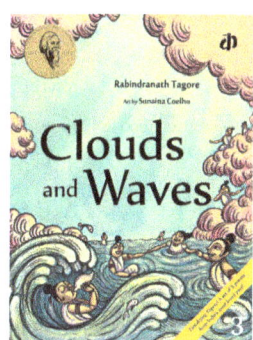

Clouds and Waves
Art by Sunaina Coelho

An endearing poem of a child who refuses tempting invitations, instead staying with her mother at playtime, blissful in her company. It is a gentle verse for little ones and their mothers!

"A sweet little tale conveying the tender love ... The inquisitiveness of the little girl, her full-of-life twinkling eyes and the tender affectionate bond that she shares with her mother are brilliantly captured by the illustrator Sunaina Coelho." — **Saffron Tree**

The Astronomer
Art by Harshvardhan Kadam

Have you ever tried to catch the Moon? Is it really that far away? Meet a little girl who doesn't think so, even as her elder brother keeps calling her silly! Decide who is right, as you follow their story.

Catch the Moon through their eyes, in this fun-filled poem by Nobel Laureate, Rabindranath Tagore.

The Champa Flower
Art by Jaikar

Get a peek into a day in the life of a boy who chooses to turn into a champa flower, just for a day. Will his mother recognize him?

A playful poem from Tagore's classic book, *The Crescent Moon*, this story is the perfect introduction for your child, to the writings of India's most famous poet.

www.ingramcontent.com/pod-product-compliance
Lightning Source LLC
Chambersburg PA
CBHW041437040426
42453CB00020B/2450

Gurudev's early education was imparted at home. In school, while others used to learn their lessons, he would slip into an exciting world of dreams. Hoping that his tutor would not come when it rained, he would sit by the window waiting. However as fate would have it his tutor's umbrella could be seen right from the corner of the road at the usual time.

Tagore wrote his first poem when he was eight. At the age of sixteen, his first book of poems was published. Aside from words and drama, his other great love was music. He composed more than two thousand songs, both the music and lyrics. He held great love and respect for children. His first poem for children was The Rainy Day.

Since childhood he loved and appreciated nature. Tagore felt that learning should be based on real life experiences and wanted to spread this message. He always believed that education is the freedom of imagination. In 1901, he founded an international university called Shantiniketan or Abode of Peace, which brought out priceless talents like Indira Gandhi, Satyajit Ray and Amartya Sen.

He has also written Aamaar Saunar Bangla, the national anthem for Bangladesh. In appreciation of all his work, Gandhiji lovingly gave him the title, Gurudev. In his last days he developed an interest in painting. In 1913 he was awarded the Nobel Prize in Literature.

Debasmita Dasgupta does social campaigns for nonprofit organizations. She loves illustrating for children's books and has a special interest in cinema, theatre and music. Currently she lives in Singapore.

Himanjali Sankar did her MPhil in English Literature from JNU. She is a senior editor with a children's publishing house and has written two children's books, *The Magical Adventures of Skinny Scribbles* and *The Stupendous Timetelling Superdog*.

Geeta Dharmarajan loves writing stories for children. She was earlier one of the editors of *Target*, a magazine for children and *The Pennsylvania Gazette*, the magazine of University of Pennsylvania. She is the Chairman of the National Bal Bhavan. She has been awarded the prestigious Padma Shri in 2012, for her distinguished service in Literature and Education.

KATHA

First published © Katha, 2013
Copyright © Katha, 2013
Text copyright © Katha, 2013
Illustrations copyright © Debasmita Dasgupta, 2011
All rights reserved. No part of this book may be reproduced or utilized in any form without the prior written permission of the publisher.
ISBN 978-93-82454-10-6
E-mail: marketing@katha.org, Website: www.katha.org

KATHA is a registered nonprofit organization devoted to enhancing the joys of reading amongst children and adults. Katha Schools are situated in the slums and streets of Delhi and tribal villages of Arunachal Pradesh.

A3 Sarvodaya Enclave, Sri Aurobindo Marg, New Delhi 110 017
Phone: 4141 6600 . 4182 9998 . 2652 1752
Fax: 2651 4373

English Translation: Himanjali Sankar and Geeta Dharmarajan

Ten per cent of sales proceeds from this book will support the quality education of children studying in Katha schools. Katha regularly plants trees to replace the wood used in the making of its books.

Tantalizing Tagore!
The other books in the series

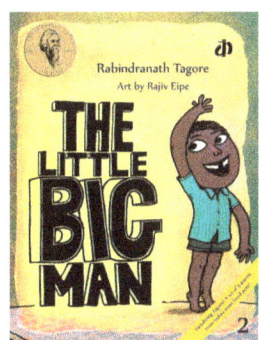

The Little Big Man
Art by Rajiv Eipe

The Little Big Man shows what it's like for a child to wear his father's shoes, to grow up and assume adult responsibilities. Through the eyes of a child, a poetic ideal!

"The artwork by Rajiv Eipe perfectly compliments the text. The little boy with front tooth missing looks absolutely endearing in his expression of – all grown up and responsible." — **Saffron Tree**

Clouds and Waves
Art by Sunaina Coelho

An endearing poem of a child who refuses tempting invitations, instead staying with her mother at playtime, blissful in her company. It is a gentle verse for little ones and their mothers!

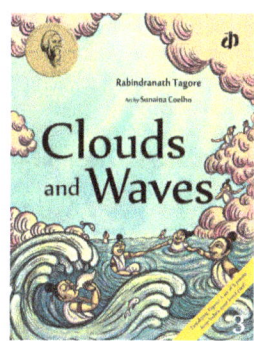

"A sweet little tale conveying the tender love ... The inquisitiveness of the little girl, her full-of-life twinkling eyes and the tender affectionate bond that she shares with her mother are brilliantly captured by the illustrator Sunaina Coelho." — **Saffron Tree**

The Astronomer
Art by Harshvardhan Kadam

Have you ever tried to catch the Moon? Is it really that far away? Meet a little girl who doesn't think so, even as her elder brother keeps calling her silly! Decide who is right, as you follow their story.

Catch the Moon through their eyes, in this fun-filled poem by Nobel Laureate, Rabindranath Tagore.

The Champa Flower
Art by Jaikar

Get a peek into a day in the life of a boy who chooses to turn into a champa flower, just for a day. Will his mother recognize him?

A playful poem from Tagore's classic book, *The Crescent Moon*, this story is the perfect introduction for your child, to the writings of India's most famous poet.

www.ingramcontent.com/pod-product-compliance
Lightning Source LLC
Chambersburg PA
CBHW041437040426
42453CB00020B/2450